T0064224

I Miss Myself

I Miss Myself

Jorge Piña

Order this book online at www.trafford.com
or email orders@trafford.com

Most Trafford titles are also available at major online book retailers.

Translated By: Elena Kúsulas Bastien

Print information available on the last page.

ISBN: 978-1-4907-6275-3 (sc)
ISBN: 978-1-4907-6276-0 (hc)
ISBN: 978-1-4907-6277-7 (e)

Library of Congress Control Number: 2015911966

Trafford rev. 07/27/2015

 www.trafford.com

North America & international
toll-free: 1 888 232 4444 (USA & Canada)
fax: 812 355 4082

Contents

Acknowledge

I want to express my gratitude to God, life, and the following persons:

To Mary, my wife, for her love, company, support, and trust in our journey together.

To Mayte and Gaby, our daughters, for their comments and suggestions, for my book.

To Nina, for being patient and wise to answer all my questions and doubts about her translation of this manuscript, which she wonderfully did.

To Fred, first of all, for being my friend but also for the prologue, the revision of the manuscript and his advise.

Jorge

Prologue

At the time of this writing, it has been nearly twenty years since I first met Jorge. It was a chance meeting with him picking me up at the Mexico City Airport for a gathering of people I was to speak to that evening. Just how relationships develop or not, is a mystery to me. Over the years, from that first encounter, our relationship has grown into a wonderful friendship and given me a deep respect for the depth of spiritual and psychological ground that makes up this man personally and professionally.

Now, once again, Jorge has given us a book, *I Miss Myself,* that seems so wonderfully simple yet is so profound in what it challenges all of us individually and collectively to undertake. This challenge is contained in the meaning of *Apocatastasis,* meaning the union of the whole with all its parts.

We live in a world that is built on duality: God and the Devil, good and evil, up and down, north and south, east and west, liberal and conservative, male and female, them and us. It is a fact, if we are to give any order and structure to the world, that duality becomes necessary as we grow into our lives. The problem develops when dualities become concretized into a final truism that keep us from knowing how all divisions stem from the same Tree of Life. Unless individuals and collectives can come to see and practice this, there will always be an "us/them" duality that lays the ground for humanity to war against itself.

It is not stretching the point to state this is exactly what *I Miss Myself* lays before the reader. Though set in the context of the personal journey of Joaquin, it includes his wife, Miranda, along with Joaquin's friend and antique dealer, Leopold and his wife, Pilar, as the story unfolds. The drama centers around a mysterious box wonderfully depicted with beautiful figures and designs that captivates anyone who gives it enough respect and attention.

As a box, it carries the question of what is inside. As symbol, it represents the universal meaning of that which can't be thrown away because is something valuable and has meaning. It is that which contains and protects. It is that mysterious box that contains the forgotten history of Joaquin along with his wife and friends.

Within that container are the dramas and traumas, the forgotten dreams, the fears, the mistakes and successes that fade into the background of any one's history as time goes by. Forgotten but not lost.

To remember can be very painful, at times, but can also be very healing if we make room for these things on our individuation journey. Life is not a straight line but a succession of curves and sometimes dead ends. But continue we must. Our deep inner world, that unknown but very real part of our psyche, does not forget.

This story encourages us to stop, listen, and muster the courage to reflect back on our history in order to reclaim consciously what was once lost. What were the events and forces that have shaped me? What were my parents and theirs before them, etc., that shaped them and echoed down through the generations and landed now at my personal doorstep?

It is a subtle twist to the story that the mysterious box is found in an antique store, that place where one finds ancient items ranging from a few decades to centuries old. What must be remembered is that each of the four people who had the courage to touch the box not only were able to reclaim something lost from their personal histories but were enabled to proceed into the future freer and more whole.

For again, is that not what Apocatastasis means? To bring everything, even the evil we have experienced or done into the greater whole of our personal being and the greater fabric of life. *I Miss Myself* is no small story of four people but one that belongs to all of us. Jorge has given us a gift with this book that lays out the pattern of how to proceed with our lives, namely, to have the courage to look back in order to proceed with the future. The reader will not be disappointed.

Fred Gustafson, D. Min.

Jungian Analyst

Introduction

People come to this world with all they need to achieve their mission but, in many cases, all the baggage we carry to achieve this divine plan —which originates from the deepest part of the human soul— is not, necessarily, what others expect or wish from us or for us.

Then begins a war between what we really are, and what the group to which we belong (family, friends, society, culture, etc.) wants us to be.

Battles are fought that sometimes are won and others are lost. With this, the most important thing for individuals is that in such wars our real personalities and —most of the times— the gifts that we carry with us are altered to the point at which we are nothing like we could have been. And as if all such things were not enough, we keep on filling a sack with all those traits, virtues, and attitudes that we have left out of ourselves thus, as strange as it may sound, making the sack really heavy for us to carry.

When our sacks are full, we get depressed and tired because we use a lot of energy trying to stop that those traits mentioned above —which accompany us when we are born— regain their strength and try to release themselves from those prisons, because they have something to offer the world. As a result, a conflict, which is as instinctive as it is divine and for which it is worth fighting, is triggered.

It is not a fight of the individual against the collective rather than the collective against the truly collective, this last being nothing but God himself.

My wish when writing this book was to invite readers to think deeply about who they are and who they could have been. This is not meant to make them feel sad but to have their energy focused on integrating the parts that were taken from that original being that was once born complete.

There might be matters that seem practically impossible to accomplish. Yet, there still are many others we can fight for if we are confident that we will achieve everything that is missing from ourselves the moment we pass from this life to the next. Hence, our duty is to travel light by wearing most of our gifts and traits and leaving in the sack the least we possibly can.

Faith and courage are necessary ingredients. But before we can have access to them, we have to fulfill a condition: We must give in. Though, we should keep in mind that giving in is not the same as being defeated but accepting reality.

The story you are about to read is simply a proposal of the way in which us people may give to ourselves much of which we lacked at some point in our lives. If any of you want to join me, you are more than welcome!

The Beginning

A couple of weeks have passed since my return home from a contemplative retreat which consisted mainly in working with dreams and other images from the unconscious. Among the goals of this retreat the possibility of experimenting, psychologically speaking, an encounter with *The Other* had been brought up.

In the afternoon of the second day —of four that the workshop lasted— and the meeting was almost over, it was suggested to be open to the possibility of discovering *The Other* at a personal level. So I went straight through a road that I had gone over before in which the branches of the trees —which were mostly pines— had built a passage similar to a tunnel, changeably lighted up by hundreds of small sun beams that intersected all the way to the ground.

It was around five in the afternoon, and the rain came and went. The rain drops that had built up on the grass started to gather inside my boots and, soon, my feet were swimming in a pool of their own.

I walked for a long time and walked across new paths. I was eager to have an encounter but not quite like the one I had the day before when I met a couple of deers that were as scared as I was, because our unexpected proximity.

I went into a road that I thought would take me to the Monastery. The vegetation began to get more and more abundant with every step I took, which made me think that it was not a very traveled way, at least not by humans.

I kept on walking and found some tracks on the way, but when I arrived to a kind of wood store, I heard a growl not so far away. So, in no time at all, I turned around and moved away because I had just realized that, without noticing it, I was invading a private territory in which it seemed like guests were not really welcomed.

On my way back, I stopped at the entrance of the tunnel of branches, but I decided to take the road on the left and was amazed to see that, after walking just a few meters, I was on the top of a hill on which there was a white wooden bench that invited me to sit and enjoy the sight of thousands of leaves painted by mother nature's brush with different shades of green.

I naturally sat there while, behind my back, the foliage of the trees was dancing to the rhythm of the wind on which thousands of rain drops were traveling swiftly, with a sound so soft and so full of life that I started feeling in my chest the restlessness of the one who is waiting to hear a voice long cherished.

A feeling of deep serenity took over my whole being. I stood there seeing, listening, and smelling a vast number of scents, until I felt with an unknown intensity that I was alive and that I was not a stranger but was certain to be a part of nature. I still feel such experience within my soul today.

The moment when all he gray shades of the sky began to turn darker, I stood up to descend to where my cabin was. The night came cautiously and, trying not to scare anyone, since it is well known that, upon its arrival, some creatures on the woods prepare to rest while others come out from their hiding places to eat.

I had to turn my flashlight on to be able to walk the half a mile that separated me from the stone chapel (a forced stop before I arrived to my shelter, where I finally entered).

Darkness had taken over the territory and, knowing itself to be sovereign, it allowed the small lights coming from the fluttering lightning bugs and through the windows of other cabins to shine.

When I took my boots and wet clothes off, I put my pajamas on, lighted the fire place and sat on a rocking chair looking through a large window to the wooden balcony where a seed bed had been feeding both birds and squirrels the entire day. Suddenly, I spotted a shape slipping stealthily through the thick bars of a balustrade, and turning around as if it was looking for something.

It came little by little toward where I was and, though I do not think it could see me because the light on the outside was on, I am sure it could perceive my presence. The raccoon —for that's what it was— went back out to the balcony and quickly disappeared.

The following day during the morning meeting in which we were supposed to share our thoughts and experiences from the night before, I talked about my brief encounter. The guide of the retreat told me that animal was probably symbolizing my encounter with *The Other*. Therefore, that night I decided not to attend the meeting and deliberately sank into the rocking chair in front of the large window feeling confident that I would consciously meet with him. I waited for more than an hour until the raccoon started climbing up the balcony. He turned all around as the night before and slowly came toward where I was.

The lights were off and the glass was the only thing separating us. But I could see it clearly and felt its look through the mask attached to its face and impossible to remove because is part of its nature. It sniffed around and disappeared descending on the right side of the balcony only to appear on the other side a moment later.

The retreat ended the next day. I went back home after a trip that lasted several hours with the hope that some future event would show me the way in which my encounter with *The Other* -the raccoon and its symbolism- would reveal itself in my everyday life. I didn't have to wait long.

The process started again sometime at dawn. I got out of bed with the feeling that I was still dreaming and, even though I was certain that there were many other things going on around me, the only one that I remembered clearly was looking at an old crumpled paper (intrinsically related with receiving) containing two words: *Severiani Hanani*. I went back to bed and resolved I had to remember them the next day, since I didn't have pen and paper at hand.

The very next morning I woke up and went straight to the bathroom. As I felt the water from the shower raining down on me I remembered those words. When I had the time, I wrote them on the search engine on my computer. A link to a site containing as the only reference the words: *Bar Hebraeus. Chronicon Ecclesiasticum II*, appeared.

I carried out a further research and wrote down the reference that was marked which took me to a series of links where I searched until I found the following:

Bar Hebraeus was a Syrian Jacobite bishop. He was also a philosopher, poet, grammarian, doctor, biblical commentator, historian, and theologian who was born in Meletinen, Armenia on 1226, and died in Maragha, Iran on 1286. He was the son of Aaron, a Jewish physician converted to the Jacobite faith, hence, his name *Bar 'Ebraya*, 'Son of the Jew'.

Bar Hebraeus was called a Monophysite. I searched further and found that during the first few centuries of the Christian era things were not simple because many different tendencies emerged. These tendencies disagreed, in one way or the other, with certain details and understandings of God's nature; for this reason, those considered orthodox called those who did not share their scope heretic. The Monophysites were part of such category.

When I was exploring the main Monophysite characters and writers, there was one that caught my attention because his name was Jorge (640-724 AD). He had a vast literary education which included the Greek Fathers. He was a follower of Santiago of Edessa who had left unfinished his poem *Hexameron*; the same that Jorge completed. In this work, Santiago teaches about *Apocatastasis* (or the restoration of all things) including the destruction of hell, about which many of the Greek Fathers learned from Origen.

The word *Apocatastasis* caught my attention. I started looking for its meaning which is according to Origen himself: "When the end of time comes, all of us, sinners and not sinners, will go back to being one with God."

Such an idea was completely rejected by the more powerful and influential groups since, should it be the case, Lucifer would have to be forgiven, which was completely unacceptable for them.

So, suddenly, and because of my dream, I was making contact with an idea that emerged during the first centuries of our time. This idea is something I really identify with because I consider that the suggestion about all human beings needing to become who we were in the beginning is related to the term *Apocatastasis*. Besides, the coincidence that the name of one of the writers defending this idea of restoration of things is the same as mine is undeniable.

Therefore, under such circumstances related to my dream, I decided to go with the flow and follow the way the energy traced almost as it emerged.

I started to wonder why all this was happening to me, so I decided to look for an event that was antique and known enough to be considered as the origin of a universal pattern of the way in which human beings abandon themselves and start living in hell.

Some days later, I thought about the name Luzbel and the story about God's favorite angel, who took the path that separated him completely from his original being and that, as a punishment for his behavior, was expelled from heaven and condemned to live on Earth where he became the carrier of the predominant energy from hell. His name also changed. He was called Lucifer or Satan.

Therefore, I thought about us humans who also separate from our original beings because some authority decided so and we are sent -as well as Luzbel- to hell and finally discover, if we are aware of what is still living inside each one of us, that life is nothing but the way back to the beginning. It consists first in knowing ourselves and then, after each discovery, accepting what we will find to the best of our understanding.

I know I am taking the risk to be considered a pathological arrogant but I would like to make the most of that idea which has been transmitted and learned by many human beings.

We, sons and daughters of God were created in His image and likeness, though we will never be the same as He is. At the end of our lives, we will simply rejoin with the Original Being that we are part of since the beginning.

That *is Apocatastasis*!

The Awakening

About twenty years ago, a man opened his eyes after having slept for a very long time and, after a moment passed, he realized he was still dreaming. He was looking at himself standing on the top of a rock facing the blue immensity of the sea.

The air was blowing intensely, ruffling his gray hair and causing his clothes to swell as if they were sails. The waves, pushed by the wind, traveled rapidly, crashing against the rocks and turning into thousands of small drops that splashed the cracks on the cliff that, as wrinkles on a face, time had shaped.

The sun was halfway on the horizon. No one would be able to distinguish if it was going up into a glorious sunrise or sinking into the ocean, as if he was making way for his inseparable companion, the moon.

Suddenly, the man realized that he was holding a wooden box in his hands. It had a metal cover carved with a wide variety of tiny figures of all kinds. It contained animals and people. It was decorated with stones that, with the sunlight, sparkled with different colors that framed what seemed to be little scenes.

He looked up again and felt incredibly light. A great feeling of peace began to penetrate his whole body. There was nothing in the world that could upset him. At that moment, he felt in full harmony with himself and with the universe.

For a moment, his mind, anxious to find a clear reason for that, asked that man what was going on, but he did not answer. The joy he was experiencing was so immense that it even prevented him from speaking.

He stood there for a while, but did not know for how long because the sun was not moving and nothing changed on the scene. All of a sudden, he woke up and for a moment he doubted he was awake, but his doubts disappeared the minute he realized he was laying in bed next to his wife, Miranda, who was soundly asleep.

That joyful feeling of peace and safety lingered a little longer. He remained still thinking that, if he moved, everything would vanish. However, he turned his head to see that it was 6:45 in the morning. In a few minutes the everyday activities would start, so he could not stay in bed any longer.

He turned the alarm clock off before it started, sat on the bed, yawned widely, and scratch his head before putting his slippers on to walk to the bathroom. He looked out the window to see that the sunlight was illuminating the peaks of two magnificent volcanoes covered in snow, which embellished the landscape.

Since his mind was back on the daily activities, he started acting automatically and performed all his morning rituals: Patterns that all human beings adapt to, some more conscious than others and are, without a doubt, paths established by repetition which mark the fertile field of the brain as the course of the rivers.

Although Joaquin -that was his name- was introverted, luck had awarded him a job in which he had to interact with a variety of people, considering that he was a youth counselor at a University.

Every day, he assisted an average of twelve students that needed support and orientation on different situations with teachers, classmates, school subjects, and even with their families. The university was a few miles away from his house, so he was used to coming and going on foot.

On his way back home after a long work day, around five in the afternoon, he stopped to have a cup of coffee with the owner of an antique shop. He loved listening to the stories that his friend told him about the many items he had for sale. Some were truly unbelievable.

That afternoon, when passing by the shop of Leopoldo —his antique dealer friend— he could see that there were new items that attracted him. His friend was in the interior, taking out of a big wooden box, lots of objects which usually came from different countries. He entered the shop and moved straight to the counter.

They greeted each other effusively, as they always did, and started talking about all the details of their every day to see if they discovered something unexpected. Whenever something unusual happened, they celebrated it drinking a glass of sherry that had been kept for so long it was at risk of becoming bitter.

Their conversation went on easily but, all of a sudden, Joaquin stopped talking. His eyes opened widely. It seemed like he had seen a ghost. His friend, Leopoldo, looked at him curiously and asked him if he was feeling well, for he looked really pale.

Joaquin approached him slowly; words were struggling, in vain, to come out of his mouth. He almost stopped breathing, while his heart was beating rapidly. He was not certain of what he was looking at. He could not believe his eyes.

Right in front of him was the box he had seen in his dream! Immediately, he put on some gloves and took the box in his hands.

Holding the box in his hands made him feel like electricity was traveling through his body. He was certain this was not coincidence. Something was about to happen, but he did not have a clue of what it would be.

Joaquin asked Leopoldo: "Where did you get this? Where does this come from? Who sent it to you? How did you know of its existence? Did a customer request it? Is it antique? Is the metal cover made of gold? Are the colored stones some kind of jewels?"

Leopoldo was surprised and he replied:

"Stop, stop, stop my friend, I cannot answer all those questions at once! Something's going on with you since you saw the box but, man, what is this commotion all about?"

Joaquin answered:

"I can't believe it! I can't believe it! You won't believe this either, but I swear it's true! Oh, my God! Oh, God!" He kept going for a while until he calmed down slowly.

At that moment, a group of people entered the store, so Leopoldo left him to go and help them. After all, he had to take care of his business. When all the customers left, he went back to see Joaquin, who was more relaxed.

"Well, Joaquin, I hope you have a good explanation for your behavior, because I simply can't imagine what caused it. Did you see a ghost? Tell me, please."

"Of course I'll tell you, Leopoldo"

And then Joaquin explained in detail to him the dream he had the night before. As he was telling his story, Leopoldo himself stared with eyes wide open.

"Well, I get it now, but I can't understand how this happened."

They continued talking until the bell of the church started ringing which indicated that it was 7:00 pm, and

Joaquin's daughters –who used to have dinner with him and his wife on Wednesdays- were about to arrive at his home.

"I have to leave, Leopoldo, but we'll see each other tomorrow. Please, take good care of the box, as if my life depended on it. See you!" And they said goodbye with a firm handshake.

Joaquin arrived home and greeted his daughters who were in the kitchen with their mother cooking some food. His two sons-in-law were sitting on a couch in the living room, watching TV. They were good, well-raised, working men, who allowed people to see the love they felt for Joaquin and Miranda's daughters.

None of them had children yet, so they enjoyed the freedom of living as couples who took care of themselves and of their relationships. They got along very well and enjoyed traveling often together.

Dinner was nice and joyful. Joaquin had decided he would keep the secret about his dream, the box, and what had happened at Leopoldo's shop. He had to make an effort not to show his excitement. He'd rather be sure about what was going on before telling anybody about it.

That night before going to bed, he doubted about asking the dream maker to give him more information, or, to leave his soul to weave the threads of energy that had made the box in his dream come true. So, he kissed his wife and went to sleep.

The following day, as soon as he finished his work at the University, he went straight to the antique shop. Leopoldo seemed to be waiting for him. As soon as Joaquin came through the door without saying a word, they hurried to the place where Leopoldo kept the most valuable items. He took a key out of the pocket on his vest, opened a drawer, and took the box his friend had dreamt about.

Joaquin put on the gloves and took it gently in his hands. The unimaginable mixture of joy, tranquility, and safety took over him. It felt so nice, that he had to tell his friend about it.

Leopoldo watched him curiously, because he had never seen Joaquin behave this way before. He suddenly noticed he started feeling like his friend. It seemed like the box released a kind of energy that was particularly positive.

What followed next was that Joaquin started asking his friend the same questions he asked the night before, but he started laughing and said: "Well, I'm acting like I did yesterday. I need to be more patient and organize my thoughts not to drive you crazy with all this, right?" And the two friends laughed gladly.

"Look!" shouted Leopoldo "as soon as you left yesterday, I checked the list of all the items noted on the import permit and, the most unbelievable thing happened! The box from your dream is not there. I don't have the slightest idea of how it got here!

"I didn't purchase it so I don't know how it got into the package of things I've ordered. I asked my assistant if she had requested it for one of our customers or for the teachers at the University, but she didn't either.

"To tell you the truth, Luisa has worked for me so long and I trust her so much, that sometimes I don't even look at the ordering reports. Besides, musketeers get old. They become distracted and forgetful. Has it happened to you, Joaquin?" And both burst into laughter.

This morning, Leopoldo said, I called the Customs Broker Agency to request information on what to do when an object that might belong to someone else is received by a person who is not the addressee. I was told to write a report and within eight to twelve weeks they would give a response. If nobody claimed the object -which was practically impossible- the receiver would be able to keep it. I have already sent the report. All we have to do now is to wait.

"Come on, Leopoldo! Are you serious? Is it true that you didn't request the box?"

"No, Joaquin, I didn't. I am as surprised as you are. But, you know what? I am making you a receipt for you to borrow the box, so you can take it home with you. In a couple of months we'll know if it stays with you or if you have to give it back. What do you think?"

Dream against Reality

Joaquin left his friend's store. He was walking fast because he wanted to arrive home and hold the box from his dream in his hands again.

The walk from the antique shop seemed like would never end. He sighed happily when he turned around the corner and caught sight of the porch of his house. He inserted the key as fast as he could, and, as soon as he entered, he went straight to the room that served as study and library.

That room, was the refuge to which he went every day especially when he was upset or worried. Being there made him feel completely at ease. It was his safe place.

His books shared the space with a wide collection of objects which he had acquired from places that, for some reason, he had visited. They were not crafts or anything similar. And, he answered to everyone who asked about them: "There simply is something about each of these objects that has caught my attention. It is not that I was looking for them, but, I am sure they found me!"

He wandered around the room for a while. He was certain that the box would show him the spot where it wanted to be placed.

He was pleased to see each and every object of his collection. Memories came quickly to his consciousness and suddenly, he discovered his own face reflected on the glass of a window. He saw that there was a big smile on that face.

At that moment, he knew that the table placed precisely below that window was a great spot. He put on the gloves that Leopoldo had given him and placed the box on the wire rod table with the mother of pearl surface. Then, he sat in front of the table to contemplate the box and, as it had happened before, he felt that already known mixture of joy, peace, and safety.

Later, Miranda arrived and Joaquin went out to the living room to receive her. Once he effusively greeted her, he said he wanted to talk to her about something very serious. For a moment she felt worried since she had seen that expression in her husband's face very few times. She urged him into telling her what was going on.

"Miranda, sit and listen to me. Please, don't interrupt me until I'm done and then ask me whatever you like. Something really amazing is happening to me, something that emerged from a dream."

She listened to him and though there were many times she felt like interrupting him, she controlled herself. At some point, she realized she had been left speechless by her husband's story. When he finished the whole story, the only words she babbled were: "Where is it? Where is that box?"

Joaquin stood up and took her by the hand to lead her to the library. Once they were in there, he said, "My dear wife, I'm sure you'll find it. I know it'll catch your eyes and you'll feel the positive energy it radiates! Go; take a tour around the room!"

Miranda doubted for a moment. However, she was used to what she called her 'husband's craziness', so she started walking around the room until she passed in front of the window that faced East when, all of a sudden, she thought she heard a voice calling her by her name.

She turned to look at Joaquin, wishing he had heard the voice too, but he was just looking at her with a big smile on his face. That confirmed the fact that only she could hear it. She heard the voice again saying: "Miranda, come this way. Yes, I am right here. Miranda, here, you can almost touch me."

She turned to the place where the voice came from and she was dazzled by the beauty of a small carved wooden box with a gold metal cover and a countless number of teeny-tiny figures of all kinds. It had houses, animals, and people. The stones sparkled in different colors. They framed what seemed to be really small scenes.

She stood still, looking at Joaquin's box. She was not able to articulate a word and remained that way for several minutes until her husband took her hand and brought her back to Earth.

"Joaquin, it is amazing! I've never seen something like it before! It looks magical!"

After a while, they held each other's hands while leaving the library and went to the kitchen to prepare a delicious Italian dinner that they had with a wine they had been keeping for a special occasion. They talked a bit more about the incarnation of the box from Joaquin's dream and what could happen next.

Many theories arouse, so they dove into them until the clock stroke one in the morning. Time flew. They were hypnotized by their conversation.

They got up and went upstairs to the bedroom where they began to perform their night rituals. When they finished them, they went into bed ready to get a good sleep. Joaquin recommended Miranda to stay alert in case something came up. For his part, he made a request, as he did sometimes, while he imagined himself passing through a threshold.

The dream maker listened to Joaquin's request to know more about what he had to do with the box and decided to reply to him in a very clear and unusual way.

Joaquin woke up the very next morning and could not remember clearly what he had dreamt about. He thought he might have to make his request a few more times. He knew that, after we ask for something, we have to wait for one of the three following replies: The first one is yes. Then, we are able to remember the dream or receive a sign almost immediately; the second one is no. Then, nothing happens and we are not able to remember the dream and the third is to wait a little, and requires having faith to insist.

After kissing his wife goodbye, he went down the stairs. It was already late to start his walk to the University, but he would have never forgiven himself if he had left without going inside the library and taking a look at the box. In that exact moment, he remembered his dream in which he had heard many times the word 'touch'. Wearing the gloves that Leopoldo gave him, he did.

He immediately felt as light as a feather. Many different images that were well known to him but that he had not remembered until that moment came to his mind.

I'm in a very small and dark place. I feel extremely uncomfortable because I cannot move. I hear strange noises. There's only one voice that I can identify well, but it is agitated.

I am almost unable to breathe. I try to be comfortable, but I can't find a right position. I feel desperate and, suddenly, something touches me. I hear voices that come closer and closer to me. I am scared! My heart beats faster with every second that goes by.

Without any warning, I feel something lifting me and, at the same time, I am so cold, I start shivering. Although I can move now, I cannot breathe. I feel I'm out of breath.

I'm not breathing! I'm spanked so hard, and it frightens me so much that I scream and start crying. The air is filling my lungs now.

I feel relieved, but there is a light so intense that I cannot open my eyes. I only hear weeping, voices, and laughter. Then, somebody comes, covers my whole body, and starts rubbing it. It feels strange, but nice. Now something enters my mouth and goes all the way to my throat with a big noise.

I don't know what's going on. I am really scared, considering that up until now I had been in a warm, soft, and peaceful place even though I didn't fit there anymore!

A little later, I start to feel again that warm sensation that surrounds my body and, even though I still feel scared, I enjoy it. I am being rubbed again, but am still cold. I haven't stopped shaking. I feel very tired. I want to sleep, but I'm not sure I will be able to.

I've been anxious for a while now, and soon they take me close to the voice that I know well. Something holds me tight and the feeling of having her near sooths me. I remain there for some time, until I stop hearing that sweet voice. I've fallen asleep.

Without noticing it, Joaquin removed his hand from the box and, at that point, he came back to the library. He thought a long time had gone by. He did not understand what had just happened. He looked at his watch, and, though worried, discovered its hand had moved just a few seconds.

He wondered if that would be the answer. If every time he touched the box, he would see images that are known to him, but which he doesn't remember if were part of his life. And so thinking, he hurried to the front door to start his walk to the University.

When a route is well known, you can traverse it 'on autopilot'. That is exactly what happened to Joaquin. He unexpectedly found himself before the entrance of the University.

He moved to his office acting distracted, which was something unusual of him, as he usually greeted every one he found on his way. He was a very popular and valued person. That *is* why all were puzzled and curious about what was going on with him.

His work day went on quietly; although that day, he had lots of appointments. It was mealtime already, but contrary to what he usually does, he decided to ask for food at the university cafeteria and stayed in his office.

Do not think he was sad or worried. On the contrary, he was really interested in knowing who had chosen him to live such an experience and why this opportunity was being granted to him.

When the bell rang announcing it was time to go home, Joaquin checked his appointment book and kept some files that he had gotten out during the day. He took his portfolio and closed his office. He waved his assistant goodbye. And now as he usually did, he said goodbye to all the people he encountered on his way through the halls of the university and out to the exit.

He did not stop at the antique shop because Miranda and he would meet Leopoldo and his wife, Pilar, that night to celebrate their friends' thirty-fifth wedding anniversary. They had built a very strong friendship and shared more than just similar tastes.

The four of them trusted each other. They knew a lot about each other's lives along with the good and the bad moments.

Leopoldo had promised his friends he would buy tickets to go to the theater. After that, they would go to have some dinner at a small restaurant which they used to visit on special occasions. However, on that day, he completely forgot about it as he was thinking about the box from Joaquin's dream. He asked his assistant to close the shop for him, and went to buy a pistachio ice cream in the nearby park.

When he arrived at the park, Leopoldo walked to the old ice-cream man who he had known since he was twelve, and who sold the best ice cream of the city. He greeted him and asked for his pistachio ice cream, then went and sat on a bench to enjoy it. Around ten minutes later, his cell phone rang. He took it out of his pocket and saw it was Pilar, his wife, who was standing outside the shop waiting for him and was calling him to ask where he was.

At that moment, he realized he had forgotten about their plans and apologized to her. He admitted to his wife as he walked back to the store that he had completely forgotten that she was picking him up and that he hadn't bought the tickets to the theater yet.

"Well, she said, we might still find seats."

Later, when they arrived at the theater, they found out there were not any tickets left; however, they were very lucky to find a man who approached them to offer them the ones he was about to return. Pilar and Leopoldo looked at each other; it was a struck of luck! They didn't think twice. They took the tickets and paid the man who walked away quickly.

Some minutes later, Joaquin and Miranda arrived, greeted them, and together entered the theater. The seats were in the very center on the eighth row. Joaquin told Leopoldo: "You must have bought these tickets in advance; they are perfect!" Pilar turned to look at her husband smiling now at each other knowing they were partners in crime.

Leopoldo handed Joaquin the brochure from the play. The moment Joaquin received it, he exclaimed: "Isn't it strange? I hadn't looked at the name of the play until now and it turns to be *Apocatastasis*!"

"Have you seen it?" asked, Pilar.

"No, it's not that", answered Joaquin. "You probably remember that some weeks ago, I went to a retreat. When I came back, I had a dream through which I found out the origin and meaning of this word. That was really weird for me at that point, though very important for me now."

"Really, Joaquin?" asked Pilar and Leopoldo almost at the same time.

"Yes, but you'll have to wait until dinner. The show is about to start." At that moment, they heard on the speakers: "Last call, we're starting!"

The main topic of the play revolved around the efforts of an individual to recover all the aspects of himself that he had lost. He had been looking for them everywhere without finding them. He knew he was missing something when he looked at the mirror every morning.

Alberto, which was the name of the main character of the play, felt really lonely and, despite being in contact with a great amount of people, he invariably had the feeling of not belonging. In any case, after a while the people he related to would have an attitude that bothered him and the charm would disappear. He submerged himself into a deep depression that he solved by meeting other people.

He was walking on the street one day when he bumped into a huge mirror that two men were lifting. He saw his whole self, reflected there. Although this experience was not a new one, this time it felt different. He had never seen himself this way before and didn't really like what he saw. Then, something surprising happened! A moment passed and he could perceive that the loneliness that made him suffer began to vanish.

From that moment on, he enjoyed every opportunity he had of looking in the mirror; not with veneration, self-satisfaction or admiration like the one a narcissist experiences, but with the great curiosity of discovering parts of himself he didn't know and that were easy to see in others without noticing that they reflected his own interior.

When they left the theater, and while they were waiting for their cars, they talked about how unusual the play was. They then drove to the restaurant to have some food and drink a good wine for love, the love of Leopoldo and Pilar and friendship.

A New Experience

The following morning, Joaquin woke up thinking about the conference he was organizing at the University for all the new students.

In most of the cases, the teenagers enrolled to study a degree but two or three semesters afterwards, they dropped out. A research on that phenomenon indicated that young people were influenced by others when making their decisions. They wanted to fulfill other people's expectations.

Miranda had already told him that breakfast was ready. Joaquin went down the stairs straight to the library to be in the presence of his box. He got closer to the table, put on the gloves, and touched the image of a family sitting at a table.

At that moment, he started to feel as light as a feather, and the following images came to his mind:

I am sitting in the dining room. It is two in the afternoon and my father is about to arrive. I'm dreadfully tense because I am about to reveal a secret to my family: I have been lying to them by telling them I am studying college. What I really have been doing for the last eight months is missing classes.

He was in distress, his stomach felt empty, and his hands were sweating. The wait was endless.

A door opens. My father arrives and my mother invites us to sit at the table to eat. My relationship with them is not so good. However, they don't expect the blow that they are about to receive in a few moments.

I can't stand it no more! I tell them what is going on. There is no way I can continue lying. My father looks at me with anger and disappointment. My mother does not know what to do. It seems like she feels guilty for my behavior.

My father does not say a word and keeps eating.

I am waiting to be scolded by him, but instead he stands up and goes to his bedroom. My mother follows him. My sister and I stay at the table.

It may sound strange, or maybe not so much, but I felt relieved of having confessed this, though this feeling is soon replaced by deep guilt and remorse.

"Hurry, Joaquin!" It was Miranda's voice and, along with it, he came back to the library.

I didn't talk much during breakfast. I was still impressed by the memory of that stage of my life. My wife asked me about my silence and I told her briefly about the images.

Her response was "Well, that box turned out to be revealing, don't you think? It might help me find out about situations of your life that I don't know about." Her mischievous tone and her big smile made my self-sympathy disappear and I joined her joy by laughing.

Luckily, that morning at the university was peaceful, unlike other days, because I was having a hard time concentrating and putting aside the memories evoked by the box from my dream.

I started wondering at what point in my life I became a liar, and an irresponsible young man, specially, because ever since I started going to school —and before I entered technical school— I was a brilliant student and received special awards due to my grades.

I remembered that when I was studying the last year of elementary school, there were serious troubles at home. Around then, my mother fell in a deep depression and passed her days lying in bed weeping.

At noon when my father arrived, I heard them arguing at a distance. Even if I got close to their door, I could not understand a word they were saying.

My relationship with my father was distant. I do not have a lot of memories about playing or chatting with him. He was a really tall, strong, and violent man. He had a kind of look that could be frightening for anyone but for a ten or eleven year old kid, it is dreadful and crushing.

He used to tell me that his father was like that too as if he was trying to justify his behavior. And though he mentioned in his stories all that he had suffered by such attitudes, he was repeating them with me.

I also remembered that when I was studying the last year of technical high-school, the economic situation of my family had fallen short. One day, my mother told us that my father had lost one of his jobs so we would have to move to a smaller house.

To me that was not much of a deal especially because some years before that, we lived in that house. Besides, it was close to my school. What turned out to be really painful was that, before the school year ended, we had to move to my grandparent's house.

I remember that we did not have money to hire a moving van. One day a classmate exclaimed, "Hey, Joaquin, I've seen that you are moving on the cart of the coalman!" She laughed loudly, mocking me. I felt deeply hurt.

For years, I was told we were better than others, though I never thought that was true. I knew the real situation and had friends from different social strata. In fact, for me such differences were unreal.

I remember clearly that when I heard my classmate's comment, I didn't know what to say; however, at that exact moment, I felt really angry and thought: "Someday, I'll make you swallow your words!"

From that moment on, mockery feels like a knife that penetrates my heart and opens one of my deepest wounds. Because I wasn't responsible for the economic situation of my family and, least of all, of the trouble my father was going through. I found about it much later.

After we had lived in a big comfortable house and moved to a smaller but also comfortable and functional house, we had to move to a space next to my grandfather's business.

It had a small living room in the front part and, through there, was the access to two bedrooms. These were separated not by doors but by curtains.

My parents slept in the first bedroom and my sister and I slept on the one next to the storehouse where my grandfather kept the materials for his business. There was neither a dining room nor hot water. In the mornings, before going to school, I warmed up a cup of chocolate milk on an electric grill. Sometimes, the hot weather had spoiled the milk. I can still remember its sour taste.

Around those days, my mother went to work at a children clothing store. I do not know her exact situation there, but I remember that she complained a lot about the amount of work. At nights when she arrived, she went straight to bed. Perhaps, she was still depressed. We continued to live there when I finished studying junior high school.

At that point in life, it was really comforting to me to have schoolmates that had not changed the way they treated me. Still, I had to study in high school, and I was not certain if my father would be able to pay for tuition. But then, my father found a job in a government educational institution. For this reason, he did not even ask me but he simply told me that I had to go and take an entry exam.

I finished junior-high with the best grades of my class and received an award that had been given only one time before in all the years the school had existed. I was feeling really confident about that, so, a few days later, I sat for the test. At night, my father asked my how it went and I answered, "It went OK, dad. It was easy."

A week later, he arrived home very pissed. He told me I had failed the test but, thanks to him, and because he was working there and had a good relationship with the principal, I would be accepted.

Soon, I found myself going to a school in which my classmates were more *experienced* than I was. I did not know anyone. I was called *blondie boy* and started experiencing verbal aggressions. I felt really lonely.

I did my best to adapt to the new school that specialized in technologies and which was not an option I had considered. In fact, at that age most young people do know what to study. However, that was not my case; I had not even given future a thought.

When I was about to finish the first year, I had a girlfriend. In the middle of my loneliness, she became a very important person until one night when I went to visit her. Her mother opened the door and told me she had to stay at the bank working late and that she did not know when she was coming back.

The next day she told me she wanted to end our relationship because she wanted to get back with her former boyfriend. I saw her many times with her girlfriends but never with him. I never got to know the truth but, once more I had something I loved taken away.

I finished technical education at that institution and started a period of imposed vacations. My father's job forced him to move to a different city. Our economic situation had gotten better for some months now. As a matter of fact, I had heard my mother saying we would soon leave the place we were living in next to my grandparents' home.

One-time when my father came to visit, he asked me if I knew what I wanted to study now. Of course I didn't but felt ashamed and compelled to answer. I did not want him to be angry. So, I simply answered: Business Administration.

A few days after that, my father rented a house and I was assigned to take care of it. My parents started buying furniture and they were afraid that someone would notice the house was uninhabited, and would break into it. So, every night during the following month two of my schoolmates, along with the older brother of one of them, came to the new house. As the house bar that was already there was filled with bottles, we drank one by one until we ran out of alcohol.

Drinking was a new experience for me. I had only drunk one time at the fifteenth birthday party of the sister of one of my classmates from the technical school. At that time, I drank a couple of glasses of rum, but the effects were such that I remember feeling so happy, I ran to a hump of sand next to a construction building and threw myself on it.

This time was different because, after having a few drinks, the four of us went out to walk on the boulevard by the sea. We walked for miles just to come back later.

At the end of the month, my mother, my sisters and I moved to the new house. Some friends and suitors of my older sister (the younger was one) started visiting. I became friends with some of them and *the party* went on for another month though it was a different kind of party. Now, we did not go out for a walk but we gathered every night and, with any excuse, bought liquor to drink and played serenades for their girlfriends.

My loneliness vanished along with my shyness with the opposite sex. I enjoyed myself so much until one night I received a call from my father telling me I had to move to the city where he lived. He had found a high school where I could study the subjects I hadn't at the technical school but that were necessary to study College.

Once more everything changed for me. I didn't even get the chance to talk to my father. He continued to control my life. I became less and less master of my future. In fact, I think I hadn't given the situation a thought for many years. With all those changes in my life happening so fast, I felt like the future was not a safe place for me anymore.

A good example of all this was when I was enrolled for two years in three different universities. I was admitted to the last one without knowing it because I sat to the test thinking it was for another university.

I was immersed in those memories when suddenly someone knocked on the door. It was a student in the third semester of dentistry who had asked for an appointment to receive counseling.

"Come on in, Maricruz, and have a sit. Tell me, how I can help you?"

"Joaquin, I need some guidance. I feel unhappy about what I am studying."

I just smiled and thought: *Such is life.*

Learning How to Take Distance

In the morning, Joaquin looked at the alarm clock out of the corner of his eye. It was almost eight. He got upset because it was Saturday and, on Saturdays, he did not work at the University. He stayed in bed a little while staring at the ceiling, not moving much, because he did not want to wake Miranda.

He remembered the chat he had with Maricruz about her wanting to study something else. One of the questions he had asked the student referred to the way in which she saw herself within five or six years once she finished studying. Maricruz answered that she did not imagine herself removing teeth and filling decayed molars. She told him that, in fact, she had suffered a lot because of her teeth and that, after studying some subjects in which people with low-income served as *guinea pigs*, she realized she wanted to work on something different. However, she was not sure of what she wanted.

"Tell me, Maricruz. Why did you decide to study dentistry in the first place?"

"The truth is that both my parents are very famous dentists, and, since I was a little girl, I heard them talk about how they wish one of their children followed their steps."

"So you wanted to please them, and that is why you enrolled in this degree."

"I owe them a lot, Joaquin. They are excellent parents. They have always supported me and my brother. I think that studying what they wanted me to, though they asked indirectly, is a good way to thank them and make them happy."

"But, you realize you weren't born to do that, don't you?"

"Well, yes. Though I would like you to help me find more than just that reason to continue studying and become a great dentist."

"What you are asking me to do, Maricruz, is something I wouldn't do, not for all the money in the world. The most important thing about my job is to help you face whatever keeps you from being who you really are."

"Joaquin, I am afraid I could disappoint my parents. I want them to feel very proud of me."

"Even if your own life depends on it, Maricruz"

"I feel guilty just to think about it."

"What would *you* like to study? Can you picture yourself being that?"

Maricruz smiled lightly despite all that sadness and fear with which she had started our conversation.

"I see myself drafting huge buildings, filled with light and gardens, with all the modern conveniences!"

"Well, I have to tell you something then. It'll be quite hard to place a brick, a light bulb, or a flowerpot inside anyone's mouth."

"Ha, ha, ha!" We laughed out loud.

"Your parents love you, Maricruz, and though they secretly wish you or your brother were dentists, they would feel happier knowing you are studying what you really want to. We all need, sooner or later, to struggle to build our future. There isn't the slightest doubt about it!

"I know you are thinking you've wasted three semesters already, but you are very young, and it is worth more to leave a ship that is sinking than staying in it despite knowing it has no future."

"Alright, Joaquin, I agree with you and I think you are right. It is hard to do it, though."

"Indeed, Maricruz. Most the times it is hard to be brave and let others get to really know you. In any case, the reward we get by being faithful to ourselves cannot be compared to anything. You truly see yourself as a future architect, don't you?"

"Indeed, Joaquin, and a very good one!"

"Hurry, then! My wife and I have been saving money for many years now. Sometimes we say it is to go on a trip, others to build a new house. So I'm not guaranteeing anything, but you may already have your first customers."

When Maricruz left my office, she was not able to hide her joy. It is just that people have qualities that make them skilled at some things, and clumsy at others.

Then, a voice made me jump on the bed:

"Why are you laughing Joaquin?"

"Miranda! Good morning."

"Some say that when someone laughs to himself, he's recalling his evil deeds."

"He, he, he in this case it's an exception." I told her what I was laughing about and we jumped out of bed to prepare our breakfast. Today, she had to cook because we took turns: While one took a bath, the other cooked.

When we finished our delicious breakfast, I washed the dishes while Miranda put the food in the fridge and prepared the grocery list. We needed to go to the supermarket.

That day, we had been invited to the wedding of her best friend's daughter. So, the visit to the hair parlor was a must.

Thus, after going grocery shopping, I left her doing her hair and, as such process takes long hours, I drove straight home to watch a semi-final match of a tennis world famous tournament.

When I got home, I walked straight to the fridge because I wanted to have a soft drink to quench my thirst. The box of my dream was half way to the kitchen and because I couldn't resist seeing it, I went into the library.

I did not give it much thought. I put the gloves on and extended my arm to touch it. My fingers laid on the image of some glasses and my body filled again with an intense feeling of joy, peace, and safety. I started feeling as light as a feather and the following images came to my mind:

I am sitting on a classroom. I can see my classmates. We are five or six years old, at least, that's what I think. The teacher is writing something on the board and, when she finishes, she addresses me, "Joaquin, you are a very smart kid. Read the numbers to your classmates".

I looked at the board to try to identify the numbers that the teacher asked me to read, but I couldn't see them clearly. I made a great effort to read. I squinted at the board, but nothing happened. I couldn't distinguish them. However, instead of saying I wasn't able to see them with clarity, I invented, causing my classmates to laugh at me.

The scandal was so big, the school principal, whose office was next to the classroom, appeared. I felt deeply embarrassed especially when they started singing: "He can't see! He can't see! He is blind!" while laughing really loud.

"Ding, Dong! Ding, Dong!" It was the sound of the bell that made me come back to the library. I walked to the door and opened it.

"Hello, Joaquin! Are you ready to watch the game?"

"What's up, Leopoldo? Come in, please. A moment ago I was ready, but I touched the box from my dream and the images that came to my mind made an impact on me."

Leopoldo observed his friend and quickly asked him, "Why don't you tell me about it? We can watch the game tomorrow you know they'll repeat it. Come on! Tell me! I am very curious about it!"

Then, Joaquin took his friend to the library and after both sat in a couple of comfortable couches, he told Leopoldo the following:

"You know what? After touching the box a few minutes ago, I began to remember many situations in which I felt limited by having to wear glasses. There were activities that I enjoyed a lot and, though I performed them, I kept on feeling something was missing. That was why I couldn't entirely enjoy them.

"For example, I enjoyed swimming but, when I took my glasses off, I couldn't see what surrounded me clearly. I could see the objects and people that were very close to me. Beyond a meter, everything started to get blurry.

"I liked playing soccer football, and though I was part of many teams and trained with them, I only participated in a few official games. In fact, my glasses broke three or four times because I tried to hit the ball with my head.

"Another aspect of wearing glasses was that, when I was a teenager, I was convinced that women considered it unattractive, and I started losing confidence, even though I got along really well with the girls from my junior high.

"You know that when people are young, it is common that friends argue and even fight about things. So, I was worried that when I took my glasses off, I wouldn't be able to see my opponent clearly enough to defend myself.

"It's funny, Leopoldo. On one hand, my boundaries to be able to relate to the outside world were very narrow. While on the other, the limits to my inside world were very broad in the sense that my imagination started to develop more and more to the point that I believed that the outside world, along with everything and everyone on it was as I imagined.

"Therefore, I started acting exclusively in accordance with my own thoughts, and, when things didn't go the way I had imagined them, a feeling of frustration and anger appeared.

"Do you realize, Leopoldo, that this is a childish attitude?"

"I agree, Joaquin. This behavior is characteristic of a lonely child."

"Now, imagine that a person continues acting like that when he is ten, fifteen, twenty, thirty, forty, or older. He is totally out-of-place but, if he is lucky, his friends will tolerate him. His indulgent inner self will tell him he is right though, on the other hand, his feeling of isolation is likely to become deeper.

"It is very important to tell you, my friend, that almost everyone's mind has a part that is conscious of the mistakes one makes. If the upbringing has been very strict, the mistakes will be numerous and the individual will start to ask himself if there is something wrong with him, or if he is the only one who thinks that way.

"What happened to me was that whenever I dared to check upon reality, I was hoping that at least one person would agree with me regarding what I had said or done.

However, most the times I was told I was mistaken. Therefore, I got angrier and more ashamed. These two feelings are powerful and make human beings suffer."

Time passed and the house door opened. Miranda and Pilar arrived from the beauty parlor.

"What's up, guys, How was the game?" asked Miranda.

And before any of us could answer that question Pilar exclaimed: "Let's go, Leopoldo, You have to get dressed up for the wedding!"

"He, he, he, forget it, Joaquin, we'll talk later."

"Alright, Leopoldo, just look at these hot girls we are going out with!"

They said goodbye without adding anything else. Joaquin went to take a bath and started thinking about the images that came to his mind earlier, about his chat with Leopoldo. When he was dry and was putting the shaving cream on his face, he started thinking:

I started wearing glasses when I was five. The shortsightedness blurred the borders of the objects that were farther than a meter from my eyes. The funny thing is that it extended beyond the physical plane so that making plans, seeing my life into the future to foresee the consequences of my acts, resulted in a difficult task then and for many years after.

On the other hand, and though it might sound like a fantasy, I was young when I started wishing for a formula to eliminate the pain and sadness of being conscious of my own life and the circumstances that surrounded me. However, I did not have a clue of how to achieve that.

At that time I needed my father the most. I needed an experienced person to guide me. I wanted to be better, but I did not know how! I wanted to solve my problems but I did not know the way! I wanted to stop suffering or to overcome my pain but no one gave me options! And how I needed them!

For instance, I remember that I was around sixteen and a classmate, Luciana lived near my house. One day, I visited her at her house to do homework; there I met her neighbor,

Falla, who I liked a lot. I obviously started visiting Luciana more often and I noted that Rafaela, her real name, was into me too.

One day Falla invited me to her house because there was going to be a party. I dressed up and went to the party, but, what happened was that her older sister did not leave me for a second. When I realized that she did not want me to be with Falla, I asked her why and she answered that it was because Falla's ex- boyfriend was there and he was a really jealous guy. She insisted that if I came close to Falla, that guy and his friends would punch me in the face, so it was better for me to leave.

I left then. I did not talk to anyone about it and though I wanted to go back to my classmate's home, I didn't, and I didn't come close to Rafaella again.

Now years have gone by and I can imagine the solution that the instinctive part of my soul, the one that only cares about life but not how it is lived, would have given to the situation. I can almost listen to it saying, "If I move his feelings more than a meter away from him, they will become blurry and his pain will cease."

The bad thing is that if it pushed the bad feelings away, it did that too with the good feelings, those that allow deep relationships to be built with oneself and with the others.

It casted those feelings that build love into the depths to save me, but that increased the painful feeling of isolation and void that was filled with a negative attitude. Thus, I became an antisocial, self-centered, arrogant, and lying individual who many people knew from the outside, but who I wanted to hide from myself.

When a human being is not able to have access to his feelings anymore, that space they used to fill in the conscious mind is filled with a lot of what had been pushed to the unconscious and does not even belong to him at a personal level.

In other words, his consciousness is occupied by the values and attitudes that are considered negative for the social group in which he was born —those attitudes that were casted aside and that, with time, had formed the *collective shadow.* Therefore, a kind of a possession in which the ego can do little to defend itself takes place. Satan is back!

Life gets more complicated and, when we are conscious, even if it is for a few seconds, it begins an internal and repetitive dialogue in which the individual asks himself lots of questions:

Why do I feel empty? Why can't I trust anyone, not even myself? Why do I end my relationships so abruptly? Why do I feel lonely? Why do I have the feeling of not belonging? Where is that being that I used to know? Where do my positive feelings hide? Are they still alive?

But he does find the answers.

That *is* life in hell! It is there where the human being misses all parts of himself that had been taken from him so that he can survive. It is there where love and confidence are lost in exchange from guilt, revenge, sadness, loneliness, impotence, and rage.

It is in hell where the true light is lost and lies shine. It is there where doubt dwells and the limits become blurry. It is there where insecurity and short-sightedness get more serious, and future, controlled by fear and anguish, stops being a nice place we have to reach.

There, immediate and casual pleasure emerges as a relief for pain. But for sure, it will cause us to get in a relatively short period of time exactly what we are trying to escape from.

That is why, from my point of view, there are moments in which the life instinct with which we are equipped makes us suffer more than we should by dragging to the depths of hell those who are closer to us and making them release their own demons from their unconscious.

In order for us to be able to leave such a place, it is necessary to get back to our consciousness those parts that were taken from us by society and by the moving force of life.

The task is to broaden the space of our consciousness in order for a larger amount of opposites to coexist in a complementary way.

It is no longer about which opposite is more powerful because, in fact, at the beginning both had the same amount of power and being together something suddenly happened by which they turned into a threat to one another.

The gods should know that it is only possible to see what is inside of each one, because we have been created in their own image and likeness. Thus, they have projected their own contents on us.

They would have to take back their own projections and be responsible for what appears in their consciousness. I think that the gods also have an unconscious.

If they manage to do so, that will be a different and lasting solution for all their fears. Therefore, as we were created in their image and likeness, the formula will work for us too.

A Bit of Guilt

The previous night, we had fun at the wedding. We talked a lot, ate a lot, and danced a lot. We left the party when the sun began to transform the night into an urgent sunrise.

Miranda and I did not wake up until around four in the afternoon, when the telephone rang. I answered it with a laconic "hello?" A high pitched voice asked to talk to someone we did not know, so I answered "No, ma'am, you've got the wrong number".

Of course Miranda woke up too. We sat on the bed with our hair all messy and frizzy and decided to call Leopoldo and Pilar to see if they were awake and wanted to come over and have some pizza with us.

As we live a few blocks apart from each other, our friends arrived along with the pizza deliveryman. We did not talk much because hunger succeeded in stopping our conversation. We just sat there and ate the pizza very quickly.

After a while, Pilar asked me if I had touched the box from my dream again and, if at any point, I would let her or Leopoldo do it.

Of course, Pilar! "Would you like to touch it right now?"

"Well, if it's not a problem for you, I would love to try."

"Let's go to the library then!"

The three of us sat there while Pilar walked stealthily towards the table where the box was. She put the gloves on and, extending her arm, she delicately posed her fingers on the image of a boy and a girl.

She stayed in front of the window for a little while and Miranda, who was closer to her than Leopoldo and I, heard her say something. At that point, she touched Pilar's right arm very softly. Pilar broke out in tears. She took her hand away from the box, walked towards Leopoldo and sat on his lap, resting her head on his shoulder. She was crying like a little girl and stayed like that for a few minutes. The rest of us waited curiously.

Leopoldo caressed her hair and Pilar calmed down slowly until she sat up and asked, "Where did it come from? It's a magic box! As soon as I touched it, I had a feeling of peace and tranquility that was very soothing until:

> *I saw myself when I was eight or nine years old in the study room of my uncle's house. One of his kids, my cousin, who is a young boy, has me sitting on his lap. He is caressing my legs with his hands which he takes up to my panties. He tries to move them aside and do something with his fingers, but I resist.*
>
> *I am really afraid because I fear that somebody might see us for I feel that what he is doing is not good. But at the same time, the feeling of it is nice. I tell him to take his hands off me. He says it is only a game and a secret between us. Then he warns me that when you tell secrets, something bad happens to your siblings and parents.*

Seeing those images made me get in touch with those deep feelings of shame, guilt, and impotence that I had at that time. What happens is that I didn't know how they were called then and I simply had the feeling of being dirty.

What left a mark on me was that I couldn't tell anyone. For this reason, when I became a young woman and any of my boyfriends tried to go too far when it came to caressing me, words wouldn't come out of my mouth. Instead I started to cry and they would stop and be scared."

"Pilar," said Joaquin, "do you realize that your tears were the only way in which you could express your disagreement? That's how your pain was revealed. I feel very impressed about your story."

"You know what, Joaquin? I would rather be able to tell them to stop or perhaps even slap them on the face, but my mouth didn't open and my body was paralyzed!

"In fact, it took me years to tell this to anyone. This secret made me feel deeply ashamed. Besides, I was afraid of being judged and kept on thinking that people would see me as being wrong if they listened to my story.

"One day I was chatting with Leopoldo and the topic about boundaries that sometimes prevent couples from enjoying their sexuality more freely arouse, so my husband told me about an experience he had when he was a little boy. That encouraged me to tell him about what had happened with my cousin who we occasionally see at family parties. I asked him not to say anything to him and he agreed."

"Well, I must congratulate you for sharing your experiences with each other. Miranda and I are very thankful for your trust which is, without doubt, reciprocated."

Then Pilar told Leopoldo that she was very curious to see if the box worked with anyone who touched it because it seemed to be so. She exclaimed to him, "Touch it, Leopoldo! Touch it!" And without thinking it twice, Leopoldo put the gloves on and extending his arm, he touched the image of a black bow on the box from my dream.

At that very moment his expression turned into peace that was transformed within a few seconds. The rest of us were observing, waiting, filled with curiosity about that experience.

When he took his hand away from the box, he mentioned:

A long time ago when I was eight, on a Sunday afternoon, my two sisters and I were watching TV. My father, who was a civil engineer working at a very big construction company, sat next to us and, with a sad expression, told us he had to make a job trip and that he wasn't sure when he was coming back.

The three of us were young, so we just look at each other, concerned. It was an unexpected announcement. We all felt very anxious, as we could confirm years later talking about that moment.

When our mom realized about how we were feeling, she smiled at the same time she told us not to be worried. Dad would keep constantly in touch with us. Her words calmed us down and it got better when dad told us he was going to build a very big dam with his friends and coworkers so the people who lived in the country had electricity.

Several weeks passed by and, as he had promised, we had been receiving many letters and cards from him telling us how he was doing. My mother answered all of them. In every reply, she included our questions and wishes. We missed him much. Months went on by and the three of us told ourselves that with each passing day, we had to wait less for him to be back.

One night, after we arrived home from the park and my mom was fixing our uniforms, the phone rang. My sister Rosita answered it and told my mother it was a long distance call. She picked up the phone and, after saying a few words, hung up.

I asked who was it but she said they've got a wrong number. However, as of that moment, she didn't speak a single word. During diner, we realized that her eyes filled with tears many times.

We asked her if she was sad, but she answered it was that something had gotten into her eyes.

We finished our meal and she put us to bed, blessing us as she always did. We were awake for a while, though none of us dared to say anything. We fell asleep until the sound of the telephone woke us up and we heard our mom crying inconsolably.

Leopoldo stopped; a couple of tears went down his cheeks. Pilar tried to comfort him, but he asked her to wait because he hadn't finished his story. He went on:

The three of us jumped out of bed and ran quickly to the living room where the telephone was. My mom saw us and tried to smile, but what we could see was a slight tear-stained smile on her face.

We hugged her and Leticia, my other sister, asked, 'What's going on, mom? Why are you crying? My mom answered, 'I've just been informed that your grandma died a few minutes ago'.

"When the telephone rang in the middle of the night, I had a weird sensation on my back like the one someone gets when he is really scared. My chest felt squeezed and I felt a lump in my throat. I didn't say a word. I never told anyone the thought that crossed my mind until now that I am about to tell you because you are my best friends.

I thought my father had died and felt relieved when she told us that it was my grandmother and not him. However, when I realized that, I felt rather guilty for my joy.

As minutes passed by, I started to feel deeply ashamed. A serious accusation hovered in my head. 'You are a bad boy! Good boys don't feel happy when their grandma dies!' I was thinking about that when the telephone rang again. My mother answered and tears rolled down her face again. She fell down on her knees, devastated, looking with a lifeless gaze to the infinity.

> *My sisters and I didn't know what to do. After*
> *what seemed to be like a long time, my mom looked*
> *at us and said, 'Kids, there has been an accident at*
> *the construction site, your father is in the hospital'.*
> *My heart crushed.*
>
> *The first thought that came to my mind was that*
> *it was the punishment for having been happy about*
> *my grandma's death, and the fear that I felt toward*
> *God multiplied a thousand times."*

When Leopoldo finished relating the images that came to his head by touching the box, the four of us remained silent.

Suddenly, Miranda said, "You know what? I'm the only one who hasn't touched the box yet and I think it is a good time for me to do it. I am a little scared but I have seen that all of you finish your experiences with a new look on your faces, and, despite what you have remembered, I see you at ease. That has convinced me that it'll be alright."

She stood up, and without adding anything else, put the gloves on and touched one of the small red stones on the box. The very next moment, Miranda's face showed a mix of surprise and fear. Then, it turned serious and tears fell down her cheeks. Little by little it changed again until we felt she was really calmed and saw her smile.

As soon as her hand stopped making contact with the box, Miranda opened her eyes and looked at us for a moment, then she said, "Do you want to know what just happened?"

I suddenly saw myself when I was around eleven. I had been sick with hepatitis. For this reason, I had been in bed for almost two months until one Saturday the doctor released me.

The following Monday I woke up feeling enthusiastic. I wanted to go to school and see my classmates because, despite they'd called me every day, they weren't allowed to visit me due to the fact that my illness was very contagious. I arrived early. My hair was neatly arranged, as always.

After the two first classes, I felt some discomfort in my stomach so I asked for permission to go to the bathroom. I needed to pee very badly. I hurried to the toilet and I discovered there was blood between my legs, I thought I had cut myself. I was really scared because I believed there was something wrong. I screamed so loud that some nuns and girls came running. I didn't understand what was going on. I was afraid.

When the nuns saw me, they moved closer to me and treated me with affection. Sister Anastasia took me by the hand and explained to me calmly what was going on. She told me it was a natural thing, that I was taking a big step in my life. I was turning into a young lady. Her soft voice and tender words calmed me down but, I wondered, 'Why hasn't anyone told me this would happen? Why didn't my mom explain this to me?'

After a while, I remembered that she didn't have a mother. Her mother died when she was a little baby so she grew up among men. She didn't have a woman around to talk to about her feelings and doubts.

All of a sudden, another scene came to my mind. I was standing next to my bed. I was eight or nine years old. I was slipping into my uniform and my mother was scolding me for something that I did but wasn't that important. I was frightened and sad and started crying.

Then, someone told me that the school bus was there to pick me up. I had to dry my tears and clean my face. They must not know I have cried I thought. I forgot about this incident on my way to school, while talking to my friends.

The rest of the morning I felt at ease until the bell rang indicating that it was time to go home. At that point, I started to feel really scared and anxious. I had to go back home. I wondered if my mom was still mad at me or not.

"This situation repeated many times. I was affected by it so deeply that I decided I would never do something like that to my children if I had any. I married Joaquin, had two daughters, and kept my promise. However, I have to say that at this very moment, sharing these experiences of my life with you makes me feel guilty. I feel like I'm exposing my mom.

"She died many years ago and I am certain that she loved me much though she didn't know how to express her feelings. I loved her too and I miss her. She was the essence that kept family together."

Joaquin took Miranda's hand into his and repeated what he had told her many times: "My mother-in-law and I had a very loving and respectful relationship. She always defended me and granted me a place in her family. She accepted me unconditionally. I miss her too."

Our afternoon ended along with Miranda's experience. We said good bye knowing that day we lived moments that marked our souls. We were aware that all those memories and emotions we had been keeping to ourselves had left their hiding places to heal our wounds and stopped being an invisible burden to us.

Don't Let that Day Come

Ever since the day Joaquin saw the box at his friend's shop and Leopoldo sent the report to the Customs Agency, he went to bed every night with a thought in mind he hadn't confessed to anyone, not even Miranda. At some point during the day and just before falling asleep at night, he couldn't avoid thinking the owner of the box would appear soon.

Although he tried to ignore that annoying idea, he usually couldn't until some activity made him think about something else or he finally managed to fall asleep.

On that particular morning, the idea that the owner of the box would appear soon was more intense. He spent most of the day thinking about it. His consciousness was invaded by this thought which even distracted him during an interview.

When he finished his work, he went to the antique shop where Leopoldo was unpacking new merchandise. He brought two cups of coffee to have as they chatted as they did almost every afternoon. As soon as Joaquin greeted his friend and sank into a red couch, he started telling him about the annoying image that had been bothering him all day.

When he finished his story, Leopoldo smiled from ear to ear and exclaimed, "My friend, those kinds of obsessions are not weird to me at all! Let me share something very important with you.

"A couple of years ago, I was in bed. I opened my eyes, stretched, and yawned. Pilar turned the TV on and I heard something on the news about the University I had studied at.

"They mentioned the professor that helped me with the thesis to obtain my degree. At that moment, I remembered the day I took my professional test, twenty one years after I married Pilar.

"Despite the fact that I went to the graduation party a few months before our wedding and received my diploma, I decided not to take the test. I had many reasons not to, and I'll tell you about them:

"The most important of all was that my mom had been telling me for years that there was a kind of curse in my family. Due to such a curse, not a single family member had their degree. The first time I heard that story, I kept it deep in my heart. However, when anyone asked why I didn't have my degree, I defended myself by saying that I really didn't need it. It wouldn't make me any wiser. What I needed to know, I had already learned at school.

"Another thought that worked as a reason for me was to remember those classmates that I considered less capable; those who had passed by cheating, and who had even copied my answers on tests but had their degrees already. I felt superior, so for that reason, I considered the degree to be unimportant.

The truth was that I was afraid of failing the test, and the very thought of feeling embarrassed stopped me for more than twenty years.

I clearly remember that the day of the test I arrived early in the classroom assigned for it. I saw the table and chairs disposed for the professors and my own chair. Minutes went by and, though I hadn't invited anyone, which made me feel a little confident, the professors weren't there yet. It was two or three minutes before the time and no one was there.

I stood up and walked down the corridor wondering why they weren't there yet. I wasn't able to find any of the professors so I went back to the classroom. My heart was beating so fast I thought it would come out of my chest and my hands were sweating badly. I wanted to run away. Anxiety was killing me.

Suddenly, the door opened and the professors came in. I was told that one of them used to look down on the students. It was exactly him who, taking his seat, asked me:

"Are you nervous, Leopoldo?"

"Yes, doctor, very much."

"Well, let me tell you that no one here knows more about your thesis than you do."

I was asked plenty of questions. The test took longer than an hour. Then, I was asked to leave the room so they could confer. At that time, I was almost sure that I had passed the test, though there was a slight doubt in my mind.

The door opened a few minutes later, I was invited in. I was about to sit on my chair, but the president of the jury and the other professors stood up and asked me to stand up too. Then, he exclaimed, "Mr., you are a graduate now! You heard me, you have passed the test!"

I cannot describe the joy I felt. My heart was about to explode. I was tremendously happy for having overcome such a difficult moment. I was really proud of myself. And a thought crossed my mind at that exact moment: 'The curse is broken!'

I said goodbye, took the papers that proved
I had taken the test, and went with my thesis
advisor to grab something to eat.

"Some days after the test, I discovered myself thinking about many people. Now I felt superior to all of them. So the curse of the degree was broken, but I had to struggle with this other curse: *I felt superior.* I had a hard time thinking of myself as one of many other people with my own virtues and vices. I continued to compare myself to others to find something that placed me on a higher place, notwithstanding their social or economic status.

Pride, which is nothing more than a way to defend ourselves from the deep pain of not being able to acknowledge our own value, was a common aspect of my personality. This is why I had been competing against everyone at everything until one day my dear analyst, Maria, told me to compete, but on a same level challenge. So I asked:

'How can I do that? What do you mean, Maria?'

'If you compete against those who have a better status than you, whether it is social or economic, for sure you will lose against them and you'll live angry at them and at yourself.

'Compete, if that's what you want to, but against those who are at the same level as you are. That way you'll have the same possibilities of winning.'

"She also explained to me that pride causes people who are not used to being complimented to feel an intense embarrassment combined with joy when others applaud something they say or do. These people may cry or may contain their tears. But when they cry, that is the sign that indicates a soul has been healed.

"¿You know what, Joaquin? Her words calmed me. I stopped struggling against what's outside my reach. I still remember a phrase I read once that said: 'If it is true, why do you worry about it? And if it is not true, why do you worry about it?'

"I told you my story because I want to suggest to you not to torment yourself by your thoughts. I also know they are not going away easily so, embrace them and, when they appear again, remember that the box came to you due to reasons unknown. We didn't even know it existed, but you were the one who dreamt about it just the night before it appeared here at my shop.

"Life is full of surprises which arrive at the right place, at the right time. Sometimes we like those surprises; sometimes we don't like them much. I assure you that this box will be with you as long as it has something to teach you. But when it stops working for you, its owner will appear. Be sure of it!

An Unexpected Visit

Today is Monday. The week begins promising Joaquin to be a very busy one since the mid-term exams begin at the University. The tests usually take place during the first hours of the day and, for this reason, the number of orientation appointments increases at this time of the year.

The origin of the box was still unknown and, after talking with Leopoldo, Joaquin began to forget that the owner would appear and he would have to return it to him.

The day was very busy indeed. It went by among orientation appointments with the youngsters. Suddenly, the bell rang indicating that it was five o'clock already. Joaquin was talking to a student and he could notice that two girls that were new at the school were waiting outside his office to talk to him.

When he finally finished working, the clock was striking 7:45 pm. He stretched, stood up, and took his jacket to head up to the exit. He walked fast because he wanted to have a cup of coffee with Leopoldo, but, when he arrived at the shop, it was already closed.

He arrived at his house and went directly to the library for he wanted to see the box from his dream. The moment his eyes set upon it, he felt that deep comfort and tranquility he felt each time he was around it. He moved close to it and couldn't help touching it. Without realizing it, he was touching the image of an engraved book.

In less than a second, he could see himself in the house where he lived with his mother and sisters when he was studying at the technical school. Teenager Joaquin was sitting on his bed looking worried.

Without any reason whatsoever, he turned his face up and looked at the door as if he had felt something. The traveling Joaquin thought for a moment young Joaquin was looking at him, but soon he realized he wasn't. So, he wondered what he had to do to communicate with young Joaquin who was no other but himself.

At that moment, traveling Joaquin listened open-mouthed to seventeen year-old Joaquin saying in a low voice as if he wanted his words to be heard only by him, but, at the same time, answering somebody else's questions:

"I don't know what I am going to study. I have no idea what I want to be! The worst thing is I'm about to finish technical college and I have to decide on something. But I don't know what!"

Traveling Joaquin thought about asking him if he had already talked to someone. He was amazed when he heard young Joaquin, who was still talking to himself, whisper:

'I haven't talked to anyone about this! I feel so lonely. I wish my father was here! I don't know who I can turn to.'

Traveling Joaquin was touched and felt sympathy for him by remembering he had experienced that situation. He would have loved to hug that boy, but he thought it was impossible to do it.

He remembered a document he had read. This document stated that if people don't get an adequate guidance, instincts will be in charge of everything and irrationality will prevail. This happens when the awareness of what is good and what is bad which is built by the rules of conduct accepted within a social group is not complete. In this case, the instincts don't recognize any authority at all.

Thus, traveling Joaquin promised himself he would find the way to help young Joaquin, although he didn't have a clue of how he was going to do it.

With that wish in mind, and without realizing it, he came back to his present reality. He found himself sitting on a couch in the library and very close to the box from his dream.

As he remembered what happened this time when he touched the box, he was aware of two things: The first was that he hadn't worn his gloves. The second, that he didn't say good bye to young Joaquin and tried to imagine what would have happened to him because it seemed like, one way or the other, he had perceived his presence.

He was comforted by the thought of young Joaquin *listening* to his promise. He stayed in the library until Miranda arrived and kissed him on the cheek. Then, she sat on the couch in front of him.

Joaquin opened his eyes. He was surprised. A smile appeared on his face when he saw Miranda was looking at him with the look of a little girl who has been mischievous.

"Miranda, Miranda! What's all these?"

"It's nothing, honey. I found sales at the mall, so, I couldn't resist. If you think I bought too many things, wait until Pilar arrives with Leopoldo. She bought a lot more stuff than I did". As she finished saying that, she threw herself into Joaquin's arms. He hugged her against his chest, caressing her hair.

"My dear wife, you cannot imagine the experience I had a few minutes ago with the box from my dream."

"I want to know every detail, Joaquin!"

As soon as he ended his story, Miranda exclaimed, "You are a very lucky guy! You are getting the chance to be reunited with yourself. It seems like time disappears for you, and I wonder who or what chose you to have such an experience. Do you think somebody else has had your box before? Do you think you have something in common with those people?"

"My dear, Miranda, I don't have the answers to such questions, though it would be only logical that it was in someone else's hands at some point."

"Would it be possible that Pilar, Leopoldo and I have the opportunity of living an experience like the one you just had? We have already traveled to the past to bring back important memories of our lives."

"Miranda, as many things in this life, faith is a key ingredient. Instead of answering your question, I want to ask you in return: Do you think it is possible?"

"You're a trickster! I'd better go and cook dinner, after that, I'll show you what I have inside those five bags, alright?"

"Alright"

As soon as Miranda left the room, Joaquin started thinking if not having worn the gloves would have influenced the fact that, unlike the other occasions, he was part of the scene and not just a witness.

He meditated about the promise he expressed to young Joaquin and wondered: "What am I supposed to do about it? I made a promise I might not be able to keep just because I felt sympathy for him. This wouldn't be the first time I commit myself to carry out a very difficult endeavor. There's something about me that makes me defend those that, for one reason, I consider weak. It's just a projection!

"I am beginning to realize that many times, when I help or support somebody, I am, in fact, defending myself. I think that is the answer to what I have to do with young Joaquin. I am aware that I don't have the power to change the external circumstances of his life but, if I did, I could change everything, even his joy and success. I might not have met Miranda and nor my two beautiful daughters. I would live somewhere else and had another job. I would be somebody else!

"So the only thing I can do is give him what he's missing and this means assuring him his life will continue and his future will be much better."

At that point, Joaquin remembered an exercise that took place during his training:

1) Remember yourself when you were eight years old and wait for an image.

2) Look at yourself and get slowly close to you.

3) Stay aware of the general situation of your life at that moment and check the feelings that appear.

4) Now, get closer to you and hug you with all the affection you are capable of feeling.

5) Tell that child firmly that everything's going to be alright. Tell him that, believe it or not, you live in the future and you know him. Tell him that, in spite of the problems that he is having, he *is* going to be happy.

6) Keep hugging him for a minute or two, until he calms down.

7) Tell him you have to say good bye and go back to your time. Assure him that you'll visit him if it is necessary.

As I remembered this experience, I was anxious for the night to arrive and Miranda to fall asleep. The moment came and I stayed in bed not moving for a while until she started snoring. Then, I got out of bed and went to the library. I needed the box to witness what I was about to do. Being with it was essential to me at that moment.

So, I started thinking about myself when I was eight years old. The image that came to my mind was of a picture in which I am wearing a white and blue stripped t-shirt.

I'm at my birthday party. I'm about to cut a huge cake. Although I am surrounded by friends, the look on my face is sad...

I decided to imagine that I was the photographer. I got closer to the child Joaquin and told him: 'I am very glad you are celebrating your eighth birthday! Is it ok if I hug you?' Little Joaquin looked at me and said, yes. I got closer to that blond and chubby boy who was wearing a quiff and around his neck, a collar that was formed by the combination of sweat and dirt for having been running around and playing. I got closer to give him the best hug I have ever given in my life. I felt an indescribable joy. He was able to feel my excitement and the affection I wanted to transmit.

I remained like that for a while, until the hug ended. He looked at me and said, 'you know what? I've never been hugged like that before! Do you know me?'

I replied, 'No, Joaquin, I don't. This is the first time I have come to take pictures of one of your birthdays. But I have a message for you from someone that loves you deeply and wants you to be very happy. He gave me the note but it seems like I can't find the paper, so I'll tell you what I am able to remember:

'Joaquin, I want you to know that I live in the future and, though it might sound unbelievable, I know you. It is very important for me to tell you that everything will be alright. You'll be very happy. Don't forget you are a good boy. I assure you that I'll visit you whenever you need me, and I'll give you another message."

Little Joaquin smiled. He was the one who hugged me now and then ran to his friends to continue playing. When I saw him getting away, I was very happy and calmed for having accomplished such an important task.

Without realizing it, I went back to the library and stayed there a little longer looking at the box and still enjoying the hug I had given to the eight year old Joaquin.

It was past midnight when I went up to my bedroom where Miranda was soundly sleeping. I tried not to make any noise while lying down next to her. It didn't take long for me to get to the land of dreaming and be given the following dream:

I'm at the house where I lived when I was sixteen. I'm headed to my bedroom to see young Joaquin but he's not there. I look for him everywhere, but I can't find him.

Suddenly, I am outside another house. He is talking to his girlfriend's mom who is telling him she had to stay at work because the bank is being audited. The phone rings and the lady went inside the house to answer it. Then, she comes out and tells Joaquin it is his mother. He picks up the phone and hears his mother demand him to go back to his house to study for a test that he has to take the following day. He wants to wait for his girlfriend to arrive, but he doesn't have the chance.

After a while, I can see him going away. He is sad and pissed because he doesn't understand what is going on. He doubts his girlfriend's mom. At that time, the most important thing of all was his relationship with the girl. He hates his own mother for ruining it for him.

He gets home and goes straight to his room to take out his notebook, ruler, compass, etc., and make a drawing which is the most important part of his test. Since it is a team work, he goes to a friend's house.

He is walking down the street, crying helplessly. I don't know how, but I appear next to him out of nowhere. He is surprised. I say, Joaquin, I just want you to know that I've known you for many years. Right now it may be difficult for you to believe me but, although you think that you don't understand anything and you feel deeply hurt, scared, and confused for not being able to see your girlfriend tonight, I can tell you that life will grant you good things!'

Joaquin looked at me feeling curious. He reached out to me and said, 'I don't know who you are, but I feel like I've met you before, I just don't remember where or when. Thank you for your words. I hope you are right.'

The very next morning, I woke up feeling anxious. I was thinking about the effects that my visit to little and young Joaquin would have. My life, I thought, would continue to be difficult. I was then aware that, at some point, I felt like I couldn't handle it no more because I had lost everything. So I gave up and, at that moment, my life started to change.

I was still in bed when I remembered the words of the photographer and of the guy I met on the street. They were right! I am a happy man now.

I stayed in bed looking to Miranda, thanking the universe for bringing her to me. Without her support, my existence would have been completely different.

The Needed Confirmation

The week proceeded with a great amount of meetings with students. I was so busy I couldn't talk to my friend Leopoldo or visit my library and touch my box which I could only see from a distance.

I didn't tell anyone about my experiences with child and young Joaquin. I was giving time to my heart and mind to take things in. Sometimes, especially after such a powerful event, it is important to be silent.

It wasn't until the following Monday, when I stopped working that much and I had taken my experiences in, that the minute I left the University, I ran to visit Leopoldo at his shop. He received me with a strong hug and invited me to sit on the red couch to enjoy a cup of coffee.

It was then when I related to him in detail what had happened to me. We asked ourselves if it was the fact that I didn't wear the gloves what made me appear next to myself in previous moments of my own life.

Leopoldo agreed that the glove matter could be the cause of that and added, "look, Joaquin, the box came to you and not me or our wives. I honestly think that only you can access to this coming and going through time and be here and there at the same time."

I agreed with Leopoldo and suggested I would try to touch the box without gloves again to see what happened. We continued chatting until it was time to close the shop. I said good bye to my friend and headed home.

I was so distracted thinking about my experience that I walked past my house and didn't realize it until I was a few blocks ahead, waiting at a traffic light to cross the street. I turned around and walked back.

Miranda was on a trip with a group of former classmates from high school that gathered every two years to visit different places. She wouldn't be back until the following week end.

When I arrived, I cooked myself some dinner. I ate fast and, once I finished, I headed to the library but stayed at the door looking at my box. After several minutes, I got close to the table where it was.

I was about to touch it and thought for a moment about wearing the gloves or not. I decided not to wear them. My bare hand reached out to the image of a man with a cup of coffee in his hand.

I suddenly saw myself sitting at the cafeteria of a hotel. I was around forty years old. I was drinking some coffee, staring at the horizon. I decided to take advantage of the fact that the place was really crowded and I was alone, so I went directly to the table where adult Joaquin was seated and asked his permission to have a seat.

The waiter came after some minutes and I ordered some chocolate and churros. While I was waiting for my food, I started the conversation telling him that I was on a trip, that despite being born in a small town, I had moved to a city about twenty years ago due to a job.

I started talking about what I remembered of the time when I arrived to the city. I talked about the places I went, the things I liked to eat, the walks around the city to get to know the places. He seemed puzzled of hearing a stranger talking about all that.

I finally caught his attention. He said, 'you know what? I am surprised because what you've been telling me about your life is very much like what happened to me when I came to live in this city.'

When adult Joaquin spoke about that, I had to make an effort not to smile, and just answered: 'It's amazing! I can't believe it!' And, as it happens when you see a movie for the second time, I wasn't surprised when a moment later I saw adult Joaquin sitting on a bed in a dark room, staring at a window through which he could see a neon light of the ad that read CENTRAL HOTEL.

He turned to where I was, but, I could quickly realize he did not see me. It was like he just felt my presence again. So I started hearing some words he was mumbling, though I wasn't able to understand them quite well.

I felt like at the same time I was with him and far from him. Soon, all my doubts vanished. I relaxed and the feelings in his heart appeared before my eyes as if I was reading them on a screen.

'I am depressed. I still wonder how I got here. It's been a couple of weeks since I left my home. I haven't talked to my wife or kids. I haven't talked to anyone, not even my friends or my parents.

'I'm having much trouble getting to my office. I still have to work there for a week and then I'll be unemployed. Nobody knows this, not any of my coworkers, not even my secretary. I have

to conceal my feelings, act as if none of this was happening.

'It's not the first time I have to live this way. I'm getting used to living a double life. I've been struggling for many years with what I have to do and what I want to do. This has become awful for me and all those who surround me. It gets harder to act properly. I do what I want to, though, it may sound crazy, don't want to do it.

'I don't have the slightest idea of what will happen to my life. I don't know which way to go to feel well. I've lost almost everything. I've never thought this time would come, but I'm here and now.'

After reading Joaquin's thoughts I started feeling very lonely and desperate. So, I thought, at that point, the only thing I could give him was what he was lacking: Company and hope to move on.

I stood in front of him and stared at his eyes. I placed both hands on his shoulders and let the tears *roll down my cheeks feeling certain that we were at different planes. What was my surprise when one of my tears rolled down his hand and adult Joaquin started crying too!*

We remained like that for a while. I knew he wasn't able to see me with his physical eyes, but he could hear me with the ears of his soul. So, I said to him, 'Joaquin, you may not believe this but I live in the future and at that place you are with your wife and daughters. Everything will be alright'.

Joaquin kept on crying a little longer, and then he prepared to go to bed. He fell asleep. After a while, I fell asleep too.

I don't know exactly how long I slept on the couch in the library but the cold woke me up. I stood up and went upstairs. I put my pajama on and fell asleep again.

I woke up the next morning wondering where I would meet myself the next time I touch the box from my dream.

Who is the Sender?

Two weeks after my experience at the Central Hotel, I started again to feel worried and my uncertainty increased. The period I had been granted to keep the box with me was about to expire. Nine weeks had gone by and we hadn't heard a word from the customs agency.

That day I was in my office. I had just finished an orientation meeting with a student. The phone rang. I picked it up. It was Miranda. She sounded worried when she told me she had something very important to say. She asked me to go straight home as soon as I finished working. I asked her what was going on, but she answered she'd rather tell me face to face.

When the bell rang, I gathered all my stuff and went home. I arrived there in half the time I usually do. I opened the door and saw Miranda waiting for me in the living room. I kissed her, took her hands into mine, and said: "Miranda, what is it that is so important you had to tell me face to face?"

She looked at me and her eyes were filled with tears. That frightened me, although I couldn't imagine what I was about to learn.

"Joaquin, I lied to you for the first time in my life! I told you I was going on a trip with some friends, but I didn't. I told you I'd left the city, but I hadn't."

I was shocked. I simply didn't know what to think.

"I'm really scared, Joaquin. I didn't want to tell you this but I can't keep it to myself any longer. It all started around two months ago when I noticed a lump on my left breast. I went to see a doctor that my gynecologist recommended. He checked me and suggested to take a sample in order to analyze it and make sure it was not a malignancy.

"I was in the hospital and had a surgery. They are supposed to call me as soon as they get the results. Joaquin, I am really scared it could be something bad."

I was static and remained silent for a minute. Then I said, "Miranda! It must have been horrible! If anyone knows what it feels to live hiding things from others it is me, and you know it well.

"I can't dare to reproach your actions, but I would rather had being with you." Then, we hugged really strongly and decided we wouldn't say anything to anyone until we had the results.

That night neither of us was able to sleep. We both stayed very still and silent until the sun came out.

The following days I went to work though I felt like a sleep-walker. I wasn't able to concentrate. I constantly remembered Miranda's face when she told me what had happened to her.

I discovered myself more than once imagining how I would feel like if something happened to Miranda. The sole thought of her not being with me made my heart ache deeply. I also thought about the reasons she had to hide something so important from me. I soon realized there are moments in which she still feels afraid of me.

I was busy dealing with my thoughts when I received a message from Miranda saying the results would be ready at five in the afternoon though she had to receive a confirmation call before going to get them. I felt very anxious. I wasn't able to get rid of the negative thoughts that came to my mind no matter how hard I tried. They insisted on taking my peace away.

The phone rang. My heart shrunk. I thought it was my wife again. I heard Leopoldo's voice greeting me and saying: "Joaquin, I got the letter from the customs agency!"

My heart started beating so strong; I could almost feel it coming out from my chest. For just a moment my mind was free from my worries about Miranda. "The letter had finally arrived".

I tried to go back to my work again, but I was really anxious. I wanted time to move fast. I constantly looked at the clock hoping time would fly, but the hands of the watch moved so slowly, it seemed like minutes were turning into hours.

All of a sudden, an alarm started. I thought I was delirious, but then I felt the ground shaking. At that moment, I realized it was a quake and remembered I am the one in charge of the evacuation plan. I forgot about my beloved Miranda and the letter about my box.

I immediately followed the rules of the plan, and, despite the confusion, screaming, running, and fear, the building was empty in less than three minutes.

We slowly calmed down and realized the quake had been mild. I called home to see if Miranda was doing well. She told me she was. We checked every corner of the building for damages and the students for injuries, but everything was fine.

As soon as five o'clock, the bell rang and I called Miranda to see if she had news on the lab results. She did not. We agreed that she would call me as soon as she heard anything.

I told her that Leopoldo had called me to let me know the letter had arrived. Miranda suggested I go and get it while we waited for the call from the laboratory. I left my office, took my jacket, and ran. Everyone was shocked I didn't say good bye. The only thing I wanted was to get to the antique shop.

When I got there, I almost ran over two ladies that were leaving the shop carrying lots of bags. Leopoldo was just behind them. He smiled at me and helped them to the car that was waiting for them at the door. He then came back in saying: "Joaquin, I've just made an excellent sale! I'm inviting you to have some dinner tomorrow night. What do you think?"

My answer was: "The letter, Leopoldo, where is the letter?"

"I have it here, Joaquin. I kept it in my office. Come, I'll give it to you."

Leopoldo put his hand into his vest pocket and took a key out. He opened a drawer on his desk and handed the letter to me.

"Good luck, Joaquin! We'll finally find out if the box is staying with you or if I have to give it back. Good luck, my friend!"

At that exact moment the phone rang. Leopoldo answered it. It was Pilar who said she had a flat tire and was in the middle of a street. He said: "I would love to stay and see what the letter says but I have to go help her".

So I left the shop and ran home. Miranda wasn't there but left me a message saying she had gone to the Laundromat because the lab results weren't ready yet. I went in the library and sat close to the box from my dream to read the letter:

Mr. Leopoldo Rosagranda Muñíz

Calle Manuel López Cotilla # 1135

Ciudad Vereda

Dear sir,

We appreciate your patience. The main reason for the reply taking this long is that we had to review the files from the last forty five years and opened more than two hundred and thirty six boxes.

We found out that this package was sent to Mr. Joaquin Pineda Quiroz on 1969; however, this person was not found at the mailing address. The package had been lost since then, and it was surprising to receive your letter saying it was inside a box we sent to your shop along with some items you had ordered.

As I told you when you talked to me in the first place, when a claim exists our protocol is to try once more to deliver the package to the addressee. For this reason I have to ask you to return it as soon as possible.

Francisco Quezada Dourell.

Executive Director.

This was just as it happened when I saw the box at Leopoldo's shop. I couldn't believe my eyes when I read my name in the letter. It meant that *I*, Joaquin Pineda Quiroz, was the one supposed to receive the package when I was seventeen. As of that moment, the most intriguing part was who sent the box.

When Miranda arrived, I went out to welcome her and told her everything about the letter. She also thought it was amazing and exclaimed: "Joaquin, we didn't expect the owner of the box to appear, but it turned out the owner *is* you! This sounds like a fairy tale!" I took her by the hand and we headed to the library.

We stood at the door for a while looking at the box on top of the wide rod table with the mother pearl top. After a while, we moved close to the table and I suggested to Miranda we touched the box together. She looked at me pensive, then, she said she was afraid just as the last time she touched it but wanted to share this adventure with me. We both touched the box on the picture of an old couple at the same time.

Soon, we were standing outside a house that looked just like ours, but was painted differently.

Miranda knocked on the door. A beautiful young lady, who was about fourteen and holding the hand of a six years old opened. Both girls were blond. Their eyes were green and bright.

"Hello", the young girl said.

"Hello, beautiful", answered Miranda.

"Who are you?" I asked.

"I'm Jimena"

"And I'm Maribel", exclaimed the little one.

We then saw a couple of old people who came to the door holding hands and smiling. She walked toward us and analyzed our faces. After that, she turned to him and said, "Joaquin, the box from your dream is magic, indeed!" We didn't need to wonder who they were anymore and, although old Joaquin didn't seem to recognize us, he invited us in.

So, we entered the house and visited every corner of it. Neither Miranda nor I could believe our eyes. The most amazing part was when they took us to the library so we could see the box on the wire rod table with the mother pearl top. Then, the old lady invited us to take a seat and drink a cup of coffee with them.

She went to the kitchen and came back with a pitcher that gave out a delightful scent. While she served the coffee in little mugs that we hadn't seen before, the old man looked for a cloth to clean his glasses.

When the four of us were finally seated, the old man took his wife's hands into his and addressed us: "Miranda, you can be sure now that your lab results were negative and you,

Joaquin, you cannot doubt the power of the box

from your dream!" Miranda and I looked at each

other and at that point we went back to our time.

We stood there, holding hands, looking into each other's eyes. We were more certain now than ever that no matter what happened we would stay together.

I took the phone and called Leopoldo to tell him he didn't need to get the senders' data. While I waited for him to answer, I imagined his face when I told him everything. But, the line went dead. He was not home.

I hung up the phone and had an urgent need to whisper in Miranda's ear, "You know what? I had never been as sure of us as I am right now." She answered, "Me neither".

The following day Leopoldo called me around seven in the morning and asked effusively, "Joaquin, tell me about the letter! What happened? Can you keep the box? Will I have to give it back?"

I replied: "Stop, stop, stop! But, man! What is this commotion all about?"

Leopoldo laughed when he heard my reply and of course I started laughing too. Finally, he said: "What happened, Joaquin? You have to tell me!"

I smiled, and answered: "Well, my friend, I'm not sure you are going to believe this but, when I got home yesterday, I opened the letter and…"

Epilogue

Dear reader, symbolically speaking we all have a box in which we keep all the parts that we have lost on our way but that, fortunately, are still inside each one of us. Those parts, together with the contents of our consciousness, form the invaluable treasure that is an almost entire being.

The map to get to them is traced in our hearts and we have access to it through the moments in which we feel left alone, frustrated, sad, angry, incapable, disoriented, and impotent.

It is good to be aware of all our wishes and of the things that we couldn't achieve throughout our lives. And, if it turns out to be impossible to take them to the outside world, we have to take advantage of our creativity and imagination.

As I said at the beginning of this book, life is a path to become who we were at first.

So, Come on! Be courageous and do it!

I assure you will stop thinking: "I miss myself"

This is *Apocatastasis*!

Explanatory Note

The term *Apocatastasis* derives from an idea that Origin coined on the first centuries of the development of the Catholic Church. He caused commotion with this idea because it suggests that, at the end of times, all of us will be one with God. If this were so, even Satan would have to be forgiven, which is, without a doubt, inconceivable.

Hence, the meaning of *Apocatastasis*: "The union of the whole with each one of its parts, without exception. It is the moment in which containment is complete, acceptance reaches its highest level, and the creation possibilities are infinite."

Apocatastasis is the moment of inspiration in which the human being contacts the deepest and timeless reality. It is the beginning and ending of all things.

If we can imagine a pendulum that is still at its lowest point, that instant which can last an eternity encloses the whole, however, it is missing something to set it in motion, a kind of energy, a sparkle, an explosion.

Human beings have named that force that is capable to move the whole:

We have called it *Love*.

Printed in the United States
By Bookmasters